HAMMERHEAD SHARKS AT RISK

SAVING THESE UNUSUAL PREDATORS

BY KATHRYN CLAY

CAPSTONE PRESS
a capstone imprint

Published by Capstone Press, an imprint of Capstone
1710 Roe Crest Drive, North Mankato, Minnesota 56003
capstonepub.com

Copyright © 2026 by Capstone. All rights reserved. No part of this publication may be reproduced in whole or in part, or stored in a retrieval system, or transmitted in any form or by any means, electronic, mechanical, photocopying, recording, or otherwise, without written permission of the publisher.

Library of Congress Cataloging-in-Publication Data is available on the Library of Congress website

ISBN: 9798875221798 (hardcover)
ISBN: 9798875221743 (paperback)
ISBN: 9798875221750 (ebook PDF)

Summary: Hammerhead sharks may look fierce, but they are at risk of dying out. Readers will learn what is causing these creatures to become endangered, including pollution, commercial fishing practices, and climate change, as well as what people can do to help.

Editorial Credits
Editor: Ashley Kuehl; Designer: Elijah Blue; Media Researcher: Jo Miller; Production Specialist: Tori Abraham

Image Credits
Alamy: Jeff Rotman, 19; Associated Press: Andre Seale/VWPics, 12; Getty Images: Colors and shapes of underwater world, 15, by wildestanimal, 7, 17, 25, Gerard Soury, 13, iStock/KTV1G1, 6, iStock/Michael Zeigler, 5, Mark Conlin/VW PICS/UIG, 9, SolStock, 28; Shutterstock: Andriy Nekrasov, 20, Benny Marty, 23 (nurse), Chase D'animulls, 23 (great white), DeawSS, 4, (heart icon) Eric Isselee, 23 (blacktip reef), Food Shop, 22, frantisekhojdysz, 23 (lemon), imranhridoy, 4, Jan Philip Morton, 29, Jsegalexplore, 26, Kletr, 23 (great hammerhead), Mark Subscenic Harris, cover, Martin Voeller, 14, nexusby, 4 (temperature icon), Rich Carey, 23 (zebra), Rob Atherton, 11 (top), Skeleton Icon, 9, 13, 17, 19, 29, (shark icon), Stefan Balaz, 4 (arrow icon), stockphoto-graf, 21, valdezrl, 27, Viktor Tanasiichuk, 11 (map)

Design Elements:
Shutterstock: Pixels Park, Textures and backgrounds

Any additional websites and resources referenced in this book are not maintained, authorized, or sponsored by Capstone. All product and company names are trademarks™ or registered® trademarks of their respective holders.

TABLE OF CONTENTS

CHAPTER 1
A DAY IN THE LIFE 5

CHAPTER 2
GET TO KNOW HAMMERHEAD SHARKS 10

CHAPTER 3
ENDANGERED STATUS 18

CHAPTER 4
CONSERVATION EFFORTS 24

GLOSSARY 30
READ MORE 31
INTERNET SITES 31
INDEX 32
ABOUT THE AUTHOR 32

Words in **bold** are in the glossary.

WHAT MAKES AN ANIMAL ENDANGERED?

NUMBER OF ANIMALS:
VERY LOW OR SHRINKING FAST

HABITAT LOSS:
BIG DECREASE IN NATURAL HABITAT

RANGE REDUCTION:
SHRINKING AREA WHERE IT CAN LIVE

BREEDING DECLINE:
FEWER ANIMALS HAVING YOUNG

THREATS:
HIGH RISK OF POACHING, DISEASE, OR CLIMATE CHANGE

CHAPTER 1
A DAY IN THE LIFE

A group of hammerhead sharks swim through the ocean's blue waters. Occasionally, they stop to search for **prey**. Their movements are swift and graceful. Powerful tails push them through strong ocean currents.

The sharks scan the seabed for fish and other small ocean animals. Their wide, flat heads look like hammers. This unique shape gives them an edge in hunting. Eyes on the sides of their heads allow them to see more of what's around them. Their wide heads also help with balance.

A smooth hammerhead shark swims near San Diego, California.

DAILY LIFE

Hammerhead sharks spend their days hunting, swimming, and resting. They often swim in groups called schools. Sharks form strong connections in their schools. Traveling together increases their chances of finding food. The schools also provide protection from larger **predators**.

A school of great hammerheads near Southeast Asia

Scalloped hammerhead sharks swim near the ocean floor.

Few ocean animals are as social as hammerheads. They use body language to communicate. They might swim in patterns or circles to attract a mate. They arch their backs to tell other sharks to stay away.

ENDANGERED

Sharks are often described as dangerous and deadly. Hammerheads are especially misunderstood. People fear their odd appearance. But hammerhead sharks rarely attack. They have a much higher risk of being harmed by humans.

They face threats from too much fishing, losing their homes, and getting caught in nets. Many kinds of hammerhead sharks are **endangered**. They could disappear forever. We need to help protect these animals. Sharks eat animals that are hurt or sick. Losing sharks would harm the ocean **ecosystem**.

Hammerhead sharks get caught in nets meant for other fish.

SHARK TRIVIA

QUESTION: How long do hammerhead sharks live?

ANSWER: Most hammerheads can live 20 to 30 years in the wild.

CHAPTER 2
GET TO KNOW HAMMERHEAD SHARKS

Hammerhead sharks live in warm coastal waters around the world. These areas include the Atlantic, Indian, and Pacific Oceans. The open areas provide perfect hunting grounds.

The largest **species** is the great hammerhead. They stay in deep ocean waters. The smaller bonnethead shark prefers shallow waters. Scalloped hammerheads swim in coral reefs. Reefs protect them from larger sharks.

Young sharks often swim in schools. Older adults tend to swim alone. They might join a school during **migrations**. Schools provide safety and better hunting.

TEN HAMMERHEAD SPECIES

There are ten different species of hammerhead sharks. Each has its own features and habitat. But they all share the hammerhead shape.

BONNETHEAD
CAROLINA HAMMERHEAD
GREAT HAMMERHEAD
SCALLOPED BONNETHEAD
SCALLOPED HAMMERHEAD

SCOOPHEAD
SMALLEYE HAMMERHEAD
SMOOTH HAMMERHEAD
WHITEFIN HAMMERHEAD
WINGHEAD SHARK

LIFE CYCLE

Sharks are fish, but most of them don't lay eggs. They give birth to live young, as mammals do. Female hammerheads have their babies in shallow waters. Young sharks are called pups. Six to 50 pups can be born at one time. Pups can swim and hunt as soon as they are born. They stay in shallow waters until they are large enough to avoid predators.

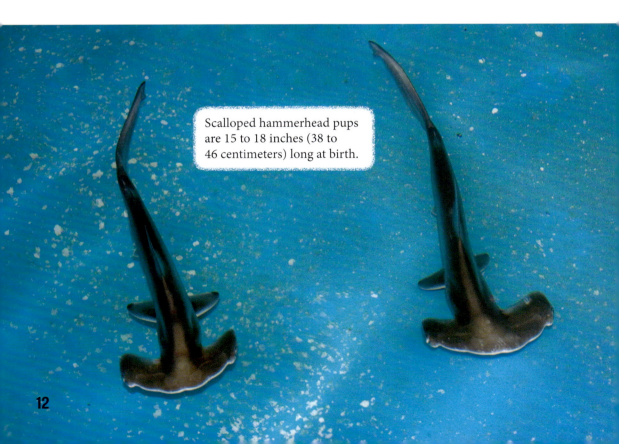

Scalloped hammerhead pups are 15 to 18 inches (38 to 46 centimeters) long at birth.

A bonnethead swims along the sandy ocean floor.

Fully grown adults weigh 500 to 1,000 pounds (225 to 450 kilograms). They can grow to 20 feet (6 meters). That's about the length of a minivan. Females are usually larger than males.

SHARK TRIVIA

QUESTION: Which hammerhead can make pups without a male mate?

ANSWER: The female bonnethead can make pups on her own!

WEAPONS AND DEFENSES

Hammerhead sharks have strong defenses to help them survive. Their sharp teeth are great for catching prey. Teeth also protect them from predators. A shark's skin is rough like sandpaper. The tough texture keeps parasites away. It helps the shark avoid injuries.

Hammerheads swallow most prey whole. But they can use their teeth to pull off smaller pieces.

Special spots on their heads can find electrical signals made by other fish. The sharks can sense the movements of animals, even stingrays hiding under the sand. The signals help sharks find food and other sharks in their school.

FOOD AND FOOD SOURCES

Hammerhead sharks need to eat often. They spend much of their time hunting. During migrations, they might travel more than 700 miles (1,125 kilometers). They migrate to find food and places to mate.

Hammerheads are **carnivores**. They feed on fish, squid, octopus, and crustaceans such as crabs and lobsters. Great hammerheads prefer stingrays. The sharks use their long, flat heads to hold the stingrays down.

Rows of sharp, triangular teeth make quick work of their catch. When a tooth falls out, a new one moves forward. Their teeth are always sharp and ready for hunting.

A great hammerhead hunts along the ocean floor.

SHARK TRIVIA

QUESTION: How many teeth do hammerhead sharks have during their lives?

ANSWER: Some sharks lose and replace up to 30,000 teeth.

CHAPTER 3
ENDANGERED STATUS

Some hammerhead sharks are endangered. They are at serious risk of disappearing completely. Their numbers are low because of a few problems. Overfishing and habitat destruction are two. Without steps to help, their population could drop even more.

Luckily, many people are willing to help protect these sharks. These efforts include setting rules on how many sharks can be caught. They also include protecting areas where they live and teaching people why sharks are important. These actions are all aimed at helping hammerhead sharks survive and increasing their numbers.

Fishers on the Gulf of California catch a hammerhead.

SHARK TRIVIA

QUESTION: How many hammerheads have disappeared in recent years?

ANSWER: Scientists estimate that some populations have decreased 80 percent in the last 70 years.

ENVIRONMENTAL RISKS

Environmental factors can also harm shark habitats and food sources. Those factors include **climate change** and pollution. Climate change can affect ocean temperatures and currents. Warmer temperatures cause prey to move in search of cooler waters. Changing water conditions can also affect breeding.

Trash sometimes ends up in the ocean. Some animals may think it is food. Eating it can make them sick.

Pollution hurts shark habitats and food sources. Garbage in the ocean harms the coral reefs that protect young sharks. Poisons in the water can cause illness or death.

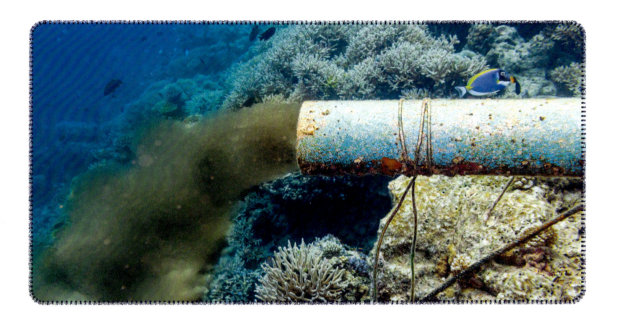

DIFFERENT LEVELS

The endangered status of hammerhead sharks is not the same for all species. Great hammerheads and scalloped hammerheads are critically endangered. Their populations have decreased by a lot over the past 10 years. The smooth hammerhead is vulnerable. Their population has shrunk. But they are not in immediate danger of extinction.

RISKS CREATED BY HUMANS

Commercial fishing is the biggest human risk to sharks. Shark fin soup is a special dish in some countries. It is considered fancy and expensive. Some people even think the shark fins have healing powers. Fishing boats catch the sharks and remove their fins. The rest of the shark is thrown back into the ocean. The shark usually dies soon after. This action is illegal in some countries, but not all.

Shark fin soup

Sharks also get caught in fishing nets meant for other fish. This is called bycatch. Sharks often die even if they are released. Injuries make it hard for them to survive.

MATCH THE SHARK

More than 500 species of sharks live in the world. Below, you'll find photos of six different sharks. Match each shark to its name.

GREAT HAMMERHEAD

A

GREAT WHITE SHARK

B

NURSE SHARK

C

LEMON SHARK

D

BLACKTIP REEF SHARK

E

ZEBRA SHARK

F

Answer Key: great hammerhead: C, great white shark: D, nurse shark: B, lemon shark: A, blacktip reef shark: F, zebra shark: E

CHAPTER 4
CONSERVATION EFFORTS

Many groups are working to protect hammerhead sharks. Some groups help local communities find ways to fish without accidentally catching sharks. Others set up protected areas in the ocean. Hammerheads can live safely in these areas. People won't disturb them.

Some places use **ecotourism** to protect endangered ocean animals. Tour groups take visitors out on boats. The groups see these sharks up close in their natural home. People learn about the sharks. They understand why it's important to protect them.

A scalloped hammerhead shark

GROUPS WORKING TO HELP HAMMERHEAD SHARKS

CONSERVATION INTERNATIONAL:
Helps people find ways to fish without catching sharks

MOKARRAN PROTECTION SOCIETY:
Studies hammerhead sharks

NATIONAL MARINE SANCTUARY FOUNDATION:
Expands protected ocean areas

SAVE OUR SEAS FOUNDATION:
Supports research and conservation efforts

INTERNATIONAL FUND FOR ANIMAL WELFARE (IFAW):
Rescues animals and rebuilds habitats

A hammerhead shark in the Bahamas

HOW DANGEROUS ARE SHARKS?

Some people don't care about saving sharks because they're afraid. They believe sharks are dangerous to humans. In reality, shark attacks are rare. Ask an adult to help you research things more dangerous than sharks. Make a picture chart to show how these dangers compare. Examples might include lightning, falling coconuts, hippo attacks, taking selfies, or falling out of bed. Add your own ideas too. Show which dangers are most likely to hurt people.

KIDS CALL TO ACTION

Kids can help protect sharks too. They can learn about them and share what they know with others. Kids can also join beach cleanups. That lowers ocean pollution.

Kids and adults can help clean up beaches. That helps keep trash out of the ocean.

Everyone can support laws that protect ocean animals and their habitats. People can avoid products made from shark fins. Doing so helps reduce the demand for shark finning. Even small actions make a difference. They help hammerhead sharks survive and swim freely.

SHARK TRIVIA

QUESTION: Which hammerhead species is smallest?

ANSWER: The small scalloped bonnethead is the smallest. It's about 35 inches (90 cm) long.

GLOSSARY

carnivore (KAHR-nuh-vor)—an animal that eats meat

climate change (KLYE-mit CHAYNJ)—a big change in Earth's weather patterns over time

ecosystem (EE-koh-sis-tuhm)—a system of living things in an environment

ecotourism (ee-koh-TOOR-ism)—visiting a place while being careful about the impact on the environment

endangered (en-DANE-jurd)—at risk of dying out

migration (mye-GRAY-shun)—traveling from one place to another

predator (PRED-uh-tur)—an animal that hunts other animals for food

prey (pray)—an animal hunted by another animal for food

species (SPEE-sheez)—a group of animals that share common characteristics

READ MORE

Crumpton, Nick. *Everything You Know about Sharks Is Wrong!* London: Nosy Crow, 2024.

Hestermann, Bethanie, and Josh Hestermann. *The Fascinating Ocean Book for Kids: 500 Incredible Facts!* Emeryville, CA: Callisto Kids, 2021.

London, Martha. *Hammerhead Shark.* Minneapolis: Bearport Publishing Company, 2022.

INTERNET SITES

Great Hammerhead Shark
saveourseas.com/worldofsharks/species/great-hammerhead-shark

Hammerhead Shark
kids.nationalgeographic.com/animals/fish/facts/hammerhead-shark

Shark Facts
conservation.org/act/shark-facts

INDEX

bycatch, 22

climate change, 4, 20
communication, 7
conservation, 18, 24–25, 28–29

ecotourism, 24
eyes, 5

fishing, 8, 22, 24, 25
food, 6, 8, 15, 16, 20, 21

habitats, 4, 8, 10, 11, 18, 20, 21, 25, 29
hunting, 5, 6, 10, 12, 16, 17

laws, 29
life span, 9

mating, 4, 7, 13, 16, 20
migration, 10, 16

overfishing, 18

poaching, 4
pollution, 20, 21, 28
population, 4, 18, 19, 21
predators, 6, 12, 14
prey, 5, 8, 14, 16, 20
pups, 4, 12, 13, 21

reefs, 10, 21

schools, 6, 10, 15
shark attacks, 27
size, 13, 29
skin, 14
species, 10, 11, 21, 23, 29

tails, 5
teeth, 14, 16, 17

ABOUT THE AUTHOR

Kathryn Clay has written more than 100 nonfiction books for kids. Her books cover a wide range of topics, including everything from sign language to space travel. When she's not writing, Kathryn works at a college, helping students develop their critical thinking and study skills. She holds master's degrees in literature and creative writing from Minnesota State University, Mankato.

Kathryn lives in southern Minnesota with her family and an energetic goldendoodle. Together, they make sustainable, eco-friendly choices whenever possible.